D0783883

![Neon sign reading TACOS BURRITOS MARGARITAS]

alphabet cooking

quadrille

Cuitlacoche
≥ 3.99

Refried
Pinto Beans
£ 1.45

M
is for mexican

recipes by rukmini iyer
photography by kim lightbody

ALLERGEN
INFORMATION
IS AVAILABLE
UPON REQUEST

M is for Mexican contains 50 of the most definitive

and delicious recipes in modern Mexican cooking.

M is for Mexican ingredients

achiote paste is a solid block of paste made from achiote seeds, vinegar, garlic and spices

agave syrup is a sweetener produced from several species of agave plant

ancho chilli is a large variety of chilli which is generally dried and has an aromatic flavour

barbacoa is the Mexican term for steamed and smoked meat

carnitas means 'little meats' and they are traditionally filled with braised pork

ceviche is a dish of marinated raw fish

chiles de arbol are a small variety of Mexican chilli pepper which are considered very hot

chipotle chilli is a smoke-dried jalapeño

chipotle in adobo is a smoky and spicy Mexican sauce

cochinita pibil is a Mexican slow-roasted pork dish

cornmeal is a meal ground from dried maze

empanadas are Mexican pastries filled with savoury ingredients

guajillo chilli are a variety of chilli pepper considered mild to hot

huitlacoche is a type of corn smut

jalapeño is a medium-sized chilli pepper considered mild to medium-hot

mixiote wrappers are made from the outermost layer of maguey leaf called penca

masa harina is the finely ground cornflour used to make corn tortillas

mulato chilli is a mild to medium chilli pepper

osso bucco is a Mexican braised veal shank dish

pasilla chilli is a dried form of chilaca chilli pepper considered medium-hot

pico de gallo is a fresh uncooked salsa made from tomato, onion, coriander and lime juice

poblano chilli is a mild chilli pepper which is often stuffed

serrano chilli is a variety of chilli pepper considered very hot

tomatillo is an edible small round purple or yellow sticky fruit

(Some Mexican ingredients are available from large supermarkets which are now starting to stock more specific ingredients. However, it is also worth checking online through suppliers such as Mexgrocer.co.uk or Mexgrocer.com.)

nida a

(street food)

a

e

jaladas

(deep fried jalapeños)

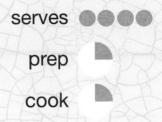
ingredients

12 jalapeños
200g (7oz/generous ¾ cup)
   cream cheese
75g (2¾oz) plain (all-purpose)
   flour
2 eggs, lightly beaten
75g (2¾oz/1 cup) fresh white
   or panko breadcrumbs

1 litre (34fl oz/4¼ cups)
   vegetable oil, to fry

cut

Wash and dry the jalapeños, then, with a knife, make a long cut along the side of each pepper and another horizontal cut close to the stem almost all the way through. Carefully remove the seeds and membrane, then stuff with cream cheese. Repeat until all the jalapeños are stuffed.

fry

Heat the vegetable oil in a deep saucepan on a medium heat to 180°C/350°F, or until a crumb turns a light golden colour within 30 seconds. Meanwhile, dip the jalapeños in the flour, then into the beaten egg, then into the breadcrumbs. Gently lower the jalapeños into the oil in batches of four, and fry for 3–4 minutes until a deep golden-brown. They are done when they reach this colour and the oil has stopped bubbling around them. Repeat until all the jalapeños are fried. Transfer to a plate lined with kitchen paper. Serve immediately.

02 gorditas
(corn pockets)

serves

prep

cook

ingredients
175g (6oz/1¼ cups) fine
   cornmeal/polenta (use masa
   harina if available)
275g (9½oz/2¼ cups) plain
   (all-purpose) flour
1 tsp baking powder
1 tsp salt
70ml (2¼fl oz/scant ⅓ cup)
   sunflower oil

3–4 Tbsp olive oil

fillings
cheese, carnitas and barbacoa
   (see pages 80 and 92), sour
   cream

mix
Mix together the cornmeal, flour, baking powder,
salt, sunflower oil and 175ml (6fl oz/⅔ cup) water
until you have a smooth dough. Cover and leave to
rest for 15 minutes.

divide
Divide the dough into 16, and flatten each into a
round cake, about 7cm (2¾in) in diameter. Cover
the cakes with clingfilm (plastic wrap) as you work.

heat
Heat 1 tablespoon olive oil in a large frying pan,
and fry the gorditas for 4 minutes on each side,
until golden brown and crisp. Transfer to a plate
lined with kitchen paper, and continue until all the
gorditas are cooked, adding more oil as needed.
Split the gorditas in two, and stuff with fillings of
your choice before serving hot.

03

queso fundido
(cheese fondue)

serves ●●●●○

prep ◔

cook ◑

ingredients

1 tsp olive oil
225g (8oz) cooking chorizo,
    chopped into small chunks
1 onion, roughly chopped
1 red chilli, finely chopped
300g (10½oz/2½ cups)
    manchego, grated
500g (1lb 2oz/3⅓ cups)
    mozzarella, chopped into
    small chunks
4 Tbsp mascarpone

handful coriander (cilantro),
    chopped, to serve (optional)
tortilla chips, to serve

fry

Preheat the oven to 200°C/400°F. Heat the olive oil in a large frying pan, and fry the chorizo on a low heat for 5 minutes before adding the onion and chilli. Fry for a further 5–6 minutes, until the onions are just softened. Set aside 3 heaped tablespoons of the mixture.

bake

Tip the rest of the chorizo and onions into a large shallow baking dish or four small ones. Pack the cheese down over the top, and dollop the mascarpone over. Transfer to the oven to bake for 20 minutes, until golden and bubbling.

serve

Scatter with the reserved chorizo and onion mixture and serve immediately with chopped coriander and tortilla chips.

tamales
(pasties)

ingredients

1 Tbsp olive oil
1 tsp cumin seeds
1 onion, finely chopped
1 tsp smoked paprika
1 tsp ground coriander
500g (1lb 2oz) minced (ground)
    beef
1 x 200g (7oz) tin chipotle in
    adobo, chopped
sea salt

250g (9oz/1⅔ cup) masa harina
    or polenta
1 tsp baking powder
½ tsp salt
4 Tbsp butter

16 corn husks

fry

Heat the olive oil in a frying pan, add the cumin
seeds and fry for a few seconds until aromatic.
Add the onion and soften for 10 minutes, partially
covered. Stir in the paprika and coriander, and
cook for a further minute before adding the beef.
Fry for 5–6 minutes until broken up and lightly
browned. Add the chipotle to the pan, along with
the adobo sauce and 200ml (7fl oz/scant 1 cup)
water. Simmer for 15 minutes and season to taste.
Allow to cool.

boil

Meanwhile, bring a large saucepan of water to
the boil and add the corn husks. Simmer for 10
minutes until soft, and then drain.

mix

For the dough, blitz the masa harina, baking
powder, salt and butter in a food processor, until
the mixture resembles fine sand. Slowly add 275ml
(9½fl oz/1¼ cups) water until the mixture comes
together into a soft dough. Remove, cover and rest
for 10 minutes.

divide

Divide the dough in half, then half again until you have 16 pieces, and flatten out the corn husks. Place a portion of dough at the wide end of each corn husk, and press it down flat over half of the surface of the husk, leaving a 2–cm (¾–in) space along the widest edge and the two long sides. One half of the husk should have nothing on it. Spoon a tablespoon filling into the centre and then, starting at the widest edge, roll the husk over the dough, folding the long edges in, continuing until the husk is completely rolled up. Secure with twine, and continue with the rest of the husks.

steam

Heat 2.5–5cm (1–2in) of water in a steamer, and place the filled tamales in the steamer basket. Steam for 30 minutes and carefully remove the corn husks before eating.

= MEXICAN FOOD

TAMALES
▶ VERDE (CHICKEN & TOMATILLO)
▶ CHICKEN & MOLE
*CONTAINS · NUTS, GLUTEN
▶ CHEESE & CHILI Ⓥ

TACOS
▶ BEEF   ▶ AL PASTOR (PORK)   ▶ VEGGIES
* ADD CHEESE £1   * * * XTRA GUACAMOLE £1

QUESADILLAS
▶ BEEF   ▶ AL PASTOR (PORK)   ▶ VEGGIES

TORTA
SANDWICH FILLED WITH EITHER BEE
CHEESE, TOMATO, ONION & L

3

£

05 empan-adas

ingredients

350g (12½oz/scant 2½ cups)
 plain (all-purpose) flour
1 tsp baking powder
1 tsp salt
85g (3oz/⅓ cup) butter, cubed
1 egg, lightly beaten
100ml (3½fl oz/scant ½ cup)
 full-fat (whole) milk

1 Tbsp olive oil
1 onion, finely chopped
2 cloves garlic, minced
1 x 400g (14oz) tin black beans
200g (7oz/1⅓ cup) feta,
 crumbled
15g (½oz)/¼ cup) coriander
 (cilantro), roughly chopped
sea salt

1 litre (34fl oz/4¼ cups)
 vegetable oil, to fry

mix

Mix together the flour, baking powder and salt
in a large bowl. Add the cubed butter, and work
together quickly with your fingertips until the mixture
resembles fine sand.

Whisk together the egg and milk, then mix it
through the flour until you have a smooth dough.
Leave to rest for 20 minutes.

heat

Meanwhile, prepare the filling. Heat the olive oil,
and soften the onion and garlic on a low heat,
covered, for 10 minutes, until soft. Stir occasionally.
Add the black beans, feta, coriander and a pinch of
salt to taste and set aside to cool.

roll

Roll out the pastry until 2mm (1/12in) thick, then
stamp out rounds using an 8–cm (3¼–in) cutter.
Reroll the extra pastry and keep stamping out
rounds until all the dough is used up – you will
have about 30.

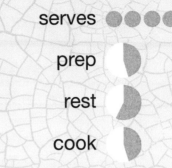

serves ●●●●

prep

rest

cook

place

Place a heaped teaspoon of the filling inside each pastry circle, brush the edges with water, then bring them together in a half moon. Pinch the edges together and use a fork to seal. Transfer the empanadas to a baking (sheet) tray lined with baking (parchment) paper and chill the filled empanadas for 15 minutes

fry

In a large, deep frying pan, heat the vegetable oil until it reaches 180ºC/350ºF or until a cube of bread dropped in fizzes and turns brown within 30 seconds. Working in batches, fry four or five empanadas at a time for 3–4 minutes, until golden-brown, flipping them over frequently to ensure they brown evenly on both sides. Drain on a plate lined with kitchen paper and continue until all are fried.

serve

Eat immediately, or warm through in the oven before serving.

06

ceviche camaron

(prawn ceviche)

serves ●●

prep ◐

cook ◑

ingredients

4 Tbsp lime juice
180g (6½oz) king prawns
  (shrimp)
100g (3½oz) cherry tomatoes
100g (3½oz) cucumber
½ red onion, finely chopped
15g (½oz/¼ cup) coriander
  (cilantro), finely chopped
1 Tbsp olive oil
1 tsp sea salt
1–3 tsp hot sauce

boil

Bring a large saucepan of water to the boil, and add a tablespoon of the lime juice. Add the prawns, reduce the heat to very low, and cook for 2 minutes before draining the prawns and rinsing them in cold water. Peel the prawns, then toss in a bowl with 2 tablespoons of the lime juice. Cover and refrigerate for 1 hour.

mix

Meanwhile, slice the tomatoes into quarters, and then in half again, and chop the cucumber into similar sized pieces. Combine with the red onion, coriander, olive oil and sea salt, and season to taste with the hot sauce and remaining lime juice.

mix

To serve, mix the prawns with the rest of the ceviche mixture and eat immediately.

07 costillas adobadas

(marinated pork ribs)

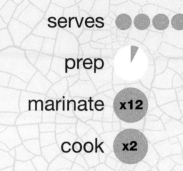

serves ●●●●

prep

marinate **x12**

cook **x2**

ingredients

2 x 500g (1lb 2oz) racks of
  pork ribs
4 tsp dried oregano
4 tsp smoked paprika
4 bay leaves
2 Tbsp sea salt
4 Tbsp olive oil
4 Tbsp white wine vinegar

mix

Mix the herbs and spices, salt, olive oil and
vinegar together in a bowl. Rub the mixture
well into both rib racks, cover and refrigerate
for 12–24 hours.

roast

Preheat your oven to 170ºC/340ºF and place the
ribs in a roasting tin. Cover tightly with foil, and
roast for 1 hour 30 minutes.

heat

At this point, you can finish off the ribs on a
barbecue, placing them on the heat until nicely
charred on both sides or, alternatively, increase
the heat in the oven to 200ºC/400ºF and roast
for a further 20 minutes until the ribs are a deep
golden-brown.

serve

Transfer the ribs to a board and slice with a sharp
knife before serving immediately.

08

flautas
(fried rolled tortillas)

serves

prep

cook

ingredients

250g (9oz) free-range
   chicken breasts
sea salt
juice 1 lime
15g (½oz/¼ cup) coriander
   (cilantro), finely chopped

1 litre (34fl oz/4¼ cups)
   vegetable oil, to fry

6 soft tortillas
4 Tbsp sour cream
1 cos (romaine) lettuce,
   shredded
pico de gallo (see page 51)

boil

Bring a large saucepan of salted water to the boil,
then add the chicken breasts. Reduce the heat
to barely a simmer and poach the chicken for
15–20 minutes, until cooked through. Remove the
cooked chicken to a chopping board and shred.
Place in a bowl and mix well with the lime juice,
coriander and 1 teaspoon sea salt.

heat

Heat the vegetable oil in a heavy-based saucepan
to 180°C/350°F or until a fragment of tortilla
dropped in fizzes and turns golden-brown within
30 seconds.

assemble

Take a tortilla and place a sixth of the chicken
mixture in the centre. Fold over two short edges,
then carefully roll it up so the filling is completely
enclosed. Use a cocktail stick to secure the edge,
then continue with the rest of the tortillas until they
are all rolled.

fry

Carefully lower two to three flautas into the hot
oil, and cook for 2 minutes, turning over halfway
through cooking to ensure they brown evenly.
Remove to a plate lined with kitchen paper and
repeat until all are cooked.

Serve the flautas immediately alongside the sour
cream, shredded lettuce and pico de gallo.

09

elote
(grilled corn)

serves

prep

cook

ingredients
4 large ears of sweetcorn
2 Tbsp vegetable oil
2 Tbsp mayonnaise
70g (2½oz/½ cup) feta, crumbled
2 Tbsp sour cream
1 tsp chilli powder
2 Tbsp coriander (cilantro), finely chopped

roast
Preheat your oven to 200°C/400°F. Place the sweetcorn in a baking (sheet) tray and drizzle with the vegetable oil. Roast for 30 minutes on a high shelf.

mix
Meanwhile, mix together the mayonnaise, feta, sour cream, chilli powder and coriander, and set aside.

serve
As soon as the sweetcorn is ready, place a couple of tablespoons of the mayonnaise mixture onto each piece of sweetcorn and smoosh it down well over each ear. Serve immediately.

(soups)

10

caldo de mariscos

(seafood soup)

serves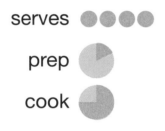

prep

cook

ingredients

1 guajillo chilli
1 ancho chilli
2 Tbsp olive oil
2 tsp cumin seeds
1 onion, roughly chopped
3 cloves garlic, finely chopped
800g (1lb 12oz) cherry
   tomatoes, roughly chopped
2 tsp dried oregano
750ml (25½fl oz/3 cups)
   fish stock
200g (7oz) firm white fish
   (cod or haddock), cut into
   3.5-cm (1½-in) pieces
200g (7oz) calamari, sliced
   into rings
200g (7oz) king prawns (shrimp)
200g (7oz) mussels, cleaned
juice of 1 lime
sea salt

toast

Toast the chillies in a dry frying pan for 2 minutes on each side, until aromatic. Deseed and transfer to a bowl of just-boiled water and leave to soak for 15 minutes.

fry

Heat the olive oil in a saucepan and fry the cumin seeds for one minute on a low heat, before adding the onion and garlic, along with a pinch of sea salt. Soften for 10 minutes, then add the tomatoes and oregano.

blend

Simmer for a further 20 minutes, stirring occasionally, then transfer to a blender, along with the chillies and 300ml (10fl oz/1¼ cups) of the fish stock. Blitz until smooth.

boil

Return the blended mixture to the pan, along with the remaining stock, and bring to the boil. Simmer for 15 minutes, and season to taste.

cut

Add the fish to the tomato broth and simmer for 3 minutes. Add the calamari and prawns, and simmer for a further minute before adding the mussels. Cook for 2 minutes until the mussels have all opened, then remove from the heat. Season with lime juice and serve immediately.

sopa de tortilla

(fried tortilla soup)

ingredients

200g (7oz) fresh vine tomatoes (3–5), halved

3 cloves garlic

2 pasilla chillies, 1 halved and deseeded, 1 deseeded and finely sliced

1 onion, cut into eighths

4 Tbsp olive oil

2 large corn tortillas, cut into strips

600ml (20½fl oz/2½ cups) hot chicken stock

sea salt

1 avocado, finely chopped

50g (1¾oz/⅓ cup) feta, crumbled

roast

Preheat your oven to 220°C/430°F. Place the tomatoes, garlic, halved chilli and onion in a roasting tin in a single layer and add 1 tablespoon olive oil and a large pinch of salt. Mix well, then roast for 20 minutes.

heat

Meanwhile, heat 2 tablespoons olive oil in a large frying pan. On a medium heat, fry the tortilla strips in batches for a couple of minutes per side, until golden-brown. Remove to a plate lined with kitchen paper, and continue until all the strips are fried. Toss with a pinch of sea salt while still warm. Add a little more oil to the pan, if needed, and fry the finely sliced chilli for a couple of minutes, until crisp. Remove with a slotted spoon to a bowl lined with kitchen paper.

soak

Once the tomatoes and onions are cooked, remove the roasted pasilla chilli from the tin and place it in the hot chicken stock to soften for 10 minutes.

blend

Remove the skin from the roasted garlic cloves, then place in a blender or food processor, along with the roasted tomatoes, onions and softened chilli. Blend until smooth.

fry

Heat the remaining tablespoon of olive oil in a saucepan and add the blended tomato and onions. Fry for 5 minutes, stirring frequently, before adding the chicken stock. Simmer for a further 10 minutes.

serve

Divide the fried tortilla strips, chopped avocado and feta between two bowls and pour the soup over the top. Serve the fried chilli alongside for people to add if they wish.

frijoles charros

(pinto bean and bacon soup)

serves ●●●●

prep ◗

cook ●

ingredients

100g (3½oz) bacon lardons
100g (3½oz) chorizo, roughly
 chopped
1 onion, roughly chopped
2 cloves garlic, finely chopped
2 serrano or jalapeño chillies,
 finely chopped
2 tsp ground cumin
400g (14oz/1⅔ cups) chopped
 tomatoes
550g (1lb 3oz/3 cups) cooked,
 drained pinto beans
500ml (17fl oz/2 cups)
 chicken stock
15g (½oz/¼ cup) coriander
 (cilantro), roughly chopped
sea salt
juice of 1 lime

fry

Place the lardons in a large saucepan and soften
on a low heat for 5 minutes, stirring occasionally to
render down the fat. Add the chorizo and fry for 5
minutes before adding the onion, garlic and chilli.
Stir, then cover and soften for 10 minutes.

add

Add the cumin and stir-fry for a minute before
adding the tomatoes, pinto beans and stock.
Stir, bring to the boil on a high heat, then
reduce the heat to medium and simmer for
40 minutes uncovered.

stir

Stir through the coriander, season to taste with the
salt and lime juice and serve hot.

13

sopa de habas

(broad bean soup)

serves ●●●●●

prep

cook

ingredients

250g (8½oz/1¼ cups) dried broad (fava) beans, soaked overnight in cold water
2 Tbsp olive oil
1 onion, roughly chopped
2 cloves garlic, finely chopped
250g (9oz) vine tomatoes, roughly chopped
700ml (23½fl oz) vegetable or chicken stock
15g (½oz/¼ cup) coriander (cilantro), roughly chopped
sea salt and freshly ground black pepper

soak

Bring a large saucepan of salted water to the boil and add the soaked beans. Simmer for 30 minutes, until tender.

fry

Meanwhile, heat the olive oil in a large saucepan, and add the onion, garlic and a pinch of sea salt. Soften, partially covered, for 10 minutes, stirring occasionally.

blend

Add the tomatoes and cook for a further 10 minutes, before pouring into a blender or food processor and blitzing until smooth. Return the tomato mixture to the pan. Drain the cooked beans and add to the tomatoes. Top up with the stock, and simmer for a further 20 minutes. Serve with coriander sprinkled on top.

14

caldo xochtil

(spicy chicken broth)

serves
prep
cook

ingredients

1 Tbsp olive oil
1 onion, finely chopped
4 cloves garlic, crushed
1 Tbsp finely chopped oregano
750ml (25½fl oz/3 cups)
    chicken stock
300g (10½oz) skinless, boneless
    chicken thighs
2 large (approx. 250g/9oz) vine
    tomatoes, finely chopped

1 avocado, finely sliced
1 green chilli, finely chopped
handful coriander (cilantro),
    roughly chopped
juice of 1 lime

fry

Heat the olive oil in a large saucepan and fry the onion on a medium heat for 5 minutes before adding the garlic and oregano. Fry for a further 5 minutes until softened.

mix

Add the stock and bring to the boil before adding the chicken thighs and reducing the heat to a low simmer. Cook for 40 minutes, partially covered. Once cooked, remove the chicken from the broth and add the finely chopped tomatoes. Simmer for a further 5 minutes.

serve

Meanwhile, shred the chicken and divide between two bowls with the sliced avocado, chilli and coriander. Pour the hot broth into each bowl and squeeze over the lime juice. Eat while hot.

caldo de chambarete

(beef broth)

serves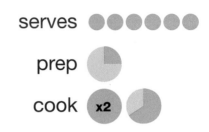
prep
cook

ingredients

1 Tbsp olive oil
1kg (2lb 3oz) osso bucco/beef
  shin on the bone
1 onion, roughly chopped
6–7 cloves garlic, halved
600g (1lb 5oz) medium
  potatoes, quartered
3 carrots, cut into 2-cm (¾-in)
  chunks
2 sweetcorn, quartered
2 courgettes (zucchini), cut
  into 2-cm (¾-in) chunks
sea salt

2 serrano or green chillies, finely
  chopped, to serve
handful coriander (cilantro) leaves
  and stems, roughly chopped,
  to serve

fry

Heat the olive oil in a stockpot and add the
osso bucco. Fry for 2 minutes on each side
until well browned.

boil

Add the onion and garlic to the pan, stir-fry for
2–3 minutes, then add 1.5 litres (51fl oz/6 cups)
water. Bring to the boil, then reduce the heat to a
low simmer, cover and leave to cook for 2 hours,
skimming the scum from the top every 30 minutes
or so.

mix

Taste the broth and season as necessary.
Add the potatoes, carrots and sweetcorn
and simmer for 30 minutes before adding the
courgettes and cooking for a further 10 minutes,
or until cooked to your liking.

serve

Remove the meat from the bones and serve with
the vegetables and broth, and a scattering of
serrano chillies and coriander leaves.

16

pico
de gallo

(salsa)

serves ●●●●

prep ◗

ingredients

350g (12½oz) fresh tomatoes,
  finely chopped
1 red onion, very finely chopped
50g (1¾oz/1 cup) coriander
  (cilantro), finely chopped
juice of 1 lime
1 red or jalapeño chilli,
  finely chopped
sea salt

place

Place the chopped tomatoes, red onion, coriander,
lime juice and chilli in a large bowl along with a
large pinch of sea salt.

season

Mix well, check for seasoning and adjust the levels
of sea salt to taste. Serve immediately.

17

guacamole

serves ●●●●
prep ◗

ingredients

2 avocados, roughly chopped
½ red onion, finely chopped
1 tomato, finely chopped
juice of 1 lime
2 tsp sea salt
25g (1oz/½ cup) coriander
   (cilantro) leaves and stems

tortilla chips, to serve

mix

Mix the chopped avocados, red onion, tomato, lime juice, sea salt and coriander together in a large bowl.

taste

Taste, and season with more salt and lime juice as needed. Serve immediately.

salsa piña picante

(pineapple salsa)

serves ●●●●

prep

ingredients
1 small pineapple
1 small red onion, finely chopped
juice of 1 lime
15g (½oz/¼ cup) coriander
  (cilantro), roughly chopped
1–2 jalapeños, finely chopped
sea salt

cut
Cut the top and bottom from the pineapple, then slice away the peel. Cut into quarters, remove the core, cut each quarter into thirds, then chop roughly into small chunks.

mix
Combine with the red onion, lime juice, coriander and jalapeños. Season with a pinch of sea salt, and serve within a few hours.

escabeche de cebolla

(pink pickled onions)

serves ●●●●

prep

cook

ingredients

1 red onion, very finely sliced
juice of 1 large lime
sea salt

cochinita pibil (see page 88),
  to serve

boil

Bring a large saucepan of water to the boil and
tip in the onion. Simmer for 30 seconds to one
minute, then drain well in a colander.

mix

Mix with the lime juice and large pinch of sea
salt. Leave to marinate for 45 minutes, stirring
once during this time. The onions will now be a
luminous pink.

serve

Check the seasoning and add more sea salt as
necessary, and serve alongside the cochinita pibil.

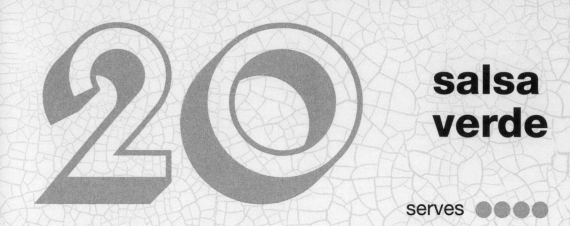

salsa verde

serves ●●●●

prep ◗

cook ◗

ingredients
300g (10½oz) tomatillos, skins
   removed
½ onion, roughly chopped
1 green chilli
20g (¾oz/generous ¼ cup)
   coriander (cilantro), roughly
   chopped
1 clove garlic, peeled
1 tsp sea salt

boil
Place the tomatillos in a saucepan of water
and simmer for 10 minutes until the tomatillos
have softened.

blend
Drain well, reserving a few tablespoons of the
cooking liquid, and transfer to a blender along
with the onion, chilli, coriander, garlic and sea salt.
Blitz until smooth. Season with more salt to taste.

serve
Leave the salsa to cool down to room temperature
before serving.

21

salsa de chipotle quemado

serves ●●●●
prep
cook

ingredients
2 Tbsp olive oil
1 onion, finely chopped
5–6 dried chipotle chillies
1 clove garlic, peeled
4 Tbsp cider vinegar
60g (2oz) agave syrup
1 tsp sea salt

heat
Heat the olive oil in a large saucepan and add the onion. Cover and soften for 10 minutes.

blend
Meanwhile, toast the chillies in a dry pan on a medium to high heat for 5 minutes per side, until almost blackened. Blitz the toasted chillies, softened onion, garlic, cider vinegar, agave syrup, 4 tablespoons water and sea salt in a blender until smooth.

Return the salsa to the pan and simmer for 30 minutes on a low heat, stirring occasionally, until very thick. Season with more vinegar or agave, to taste.

serve
Allow the salsa to cool before serving. This will keep well in the fridge for 2–3 days if covered.

22

salsa de cacahuate y chile de arbol

(peanut salsa)

serves ●●●●●●

prep ◕

ingredients

2 Tbsp olive oil
5 chiles de arbol, deseeded
1 clove garlic
150g (5½oz/1 cup) peanuts
sea salt

fry

Heat the olive oil in a frying pan and add the chiles, garlic and peanuts. Fry on a medium to low heat for 10 minutes, stirring frequently so that everything fries evenly to a golden brown.

blend

Transfer the mixture to a blender or food processor and allow it to cool down for 10 minutes. Add 1 teaspoon sea salt, and blend until smooth, adding 175ml (6fl oz/⅔ cup) water gradually as you go.

mix

Return the salsa to the pan and stir for 2 minutes over a very low heat before leaving to cool. Stir in a few extra tablespoons of water to adjust the texture as needed. Taste and season and serve alongside any of the beef or pork dishes. It will keep well refrigerated for a week in a jar.

23

salsa molcajete

(tomato salsa)

serves ●●●●
prep ◗
cook ◗

ingredients

300g (10½oz) tomatoes, approx.
3 large, on the vine
2 cloves garlic, unpeeled
2 jalapeños
1 tsp sea salt
juice of ½ lime

roast

Heat a large frying pan and dry roast the whole tomatoes, garlic and jalapeños for 5 minutes, until charred. Remove to a chopping board.

chop

Peel the garlic, remove the stems from the jalapeños and roughly chop them with the tomatoes.

mix

Using a large mortar and pestle, pound the ingredients along with the sea salt, until well broken down (if you don't have a large enough mortar and pestle to hold all the ingredients, crush them in batches). Season with the lime juice and more sea salt to taste, and serve.

24

chiltomate
(spicy salsa)

serves ●●●●
prep ▶
cook ▶

ingredients
150g (5½oz) cherry tomatoes
  on the vine
½ onion, thinly sliced
1 habanero chilli
1 clove garlic, unpeeled
2 Tbsp coriander (cilantro),
  chopped
1 tsp sea salt

heat
Heat a large griddle pan until smoking and char
the whole tomatoes, onion, habanero chilli and
garlic. After 4 minutes, turn everything over so it
can cook on the other side and griddle for a further
4 minutes. Remove to a chopping board.

blend
Peel the garlic, remove the stem from the chilli
and then transfer everything to a blender or food
processor and pulse very briefly until everything is
roughly blended.

mix
Transfer to a bowl and allow to cool down.
To serve, stir through the coriander and season
to taste with sea salt.

curtido

(pickled coleslaw)

serves

prep

cook

ingredients
2 carrots, julienned
½ sweetheart cabbage, finely
   shredded
½ red onion, finely sliced
2 Tbsp white wine vinegar
2 tsp sea salt

mix
In a large bowl, mix the carrots, cabbage and red onion together with the white wine vinegar and salt.

pickle
Cover and refrigerate for 1 hour to lightly pickle the vegetables. Taste and season if necessary with a pinch more of sea salt or a little vinegar before serving.

26

cebollitas
(griddled onions)

serves

prep

cook

ingredients
1 large bunch spring onions
   (scallions)
2 Tbsp olive oil
1 tsp sea salt
juice of 1 lime

mix
Trim the tops from the spring onions and toss with
the olive oil and sea salt in a large bowl.

char
Heat a griddle pan on high heat until smoking, then
place the spring onions on it in a single layer. Lower
the heat and griddle for 5 minutes per side, until
nicely charred.

serve
Squeeze over the lime juice and serve immediately.

27 mixiote de carneros

(spicy lamb)

serves
prep
marinate
cook **x2**

ingredients

2 guajillo chillies
2 ancho chillies
1 pasilla chillies
1 onion, finely chopped
2 cloves garlic, finely chopped
1 Tbsp oregano
1 tsp ground cumin
large pinch sea salt
400g (14oz) lamb shoulder,
    diced
4 dried avocado leaves

2 x mixiote wrappers plus foil
    (or alternatively, 2 x squares
    of baking (parchment) paper)

cooked rice, to serve

toast

Carefully slice the chillies open and press flat, removing the seeds and reserving them. Place the chillies into a large frying pan in a single layer. On a low heat, toast for 2–3 minutes until aromatic, then soak the chillies in a bowl of just-boiled water for 15 minutes.

blend

Place the soaked chillies, onion, garlic, oregano, cumin and sea salt in a blender or food processor and blitz until smooth. Add 1–2 tablespoons of the reserved chilli seeds (the more seeds the hotter it will be), along with a little soaking water if the mixture is difficult to blend.

marinate

Place the sauce in a bowl with the diced lamb, mix well and leave to marinate for at least 1 hour.

assemble

Lay out the squares of foil, and place one mixiote wrapper (or square of baking paper) on each. Place in two bowls to create 'cup' shapes, then divide the lamb mixture between the two. Top each with two avocado leaves, then twist the top of the wrappers and tie with string to seal.

mix

Bring 5–7cm (2–3in) water to boil in a steamer, and place the bundles in the steamer basket over the water. Steam for 2 hours, topping up with water, serve the lamb in the wrappers along with rice.

chicken
mole
poblano

ingredients

4 mulato chillies
3 ancho chillies
3 pasilla chillies
50g (1¾oz/scant ½ cup) raisins
50g (1¾oz/⅓ cup) almonds
50g 1¾oz/⅓ cup) pumpkin
   seeds

1kg (2lb 3oz) skinless, boneless
   chicken thighs

40g (1½oz/¼ cup) sesame
   seeds
4 cloves
1 tsp cumin seeds
1 tsp anise seeds
1 tsp peppercorns
1 cinnamon stick
2 tortillas (ideally stale)

➡ ➡ ➡

toast

Dry toast the chillies in a frying pan for 2–3 minutes
on each side until aromatic. Remove to a chopping
board, deseed and set the seeds aside. Place the
chillies along with the raisins in a bowl, cover with
just-boiled water and leave to steep for 20 minutes.

toast

Tip the almonds and pumpkin seeds into the same
pan and toast on a low heat for 5–8 minutes,
shaking the pan occasionally so they toast evenly.
The pumpkin seeds will pop, so keep a lid nearby.
Shake onto a plate to cool. Reserve a handful to
serve, then blitz the rest in a food processor until
very fine. Set aside.

boil

Meanwhile, bring 1.5 litres (51fl oz/6 cups) water
to the boil in a large pan, with a large pinch of salt,
and add the chicken. Reduce the heat to a low
simmer, and cook for 20 minutes. Drain the chicken
and reserve the stock.

serves ●●●●

prep

cook **x2**

➡ ➡ ➡
2 Tbsp olive oil
1 large onion, roughly chopped
4 cloves garlic, minced
4 tomatillos, roughly chopped

40g (1½oz/¼ cup) dark
  chocolate (70% cocoa solids
  minimum), roughly chopped
sea salt

cooked rice, to serve

mix

Drain the chillies and raisins. Tip the raisins into a hot frying pan and toast for 5 minutes, until they puff up. Set aside. Toast the sesame seeds, cloves, cumin seeds, anise seeds, peppercorns, cinnamon stick and reserved chilli seeds for 3–4 minutes until aromatic. Remove, allow to cool down, then pound using a mortar and pestle or coffee grinder. Toast the tortilla for 2–3 minutes per side, then set aside.

heat

Heat the olive oil in a pan and soften the onion and garlic together with a pinch of sea salt for 10 minutes. Add the tomatillos and cook for a further 5 minutes. Tip into the food processor, with the drained chillies and puffed raisins, and blitz until smooth.

Add the ground nuts and seeds, spices, tortilla and 700ml (23½fl oz) chicken stock to the chillies and raisins and blitz until smooth. Pour this mixture into the pan and bring to a simmer. Return the chicken to the pan and simmer for 1 hour. Stir in the chocolate after 30 minutes and season to taste with sea salt. Add a little more stock if the sauce looks too thick. Serve the mole with freshly cooked rice and a few reserved pumpkin seeds.

barbacoa

(slow-cooked beef)

serves ●●●●●

prep ◑

cook x3

ingredients

3 Tbsp olive oil
900g (2lb) diced beef
2 onions, roughly chopped
4 ancho chillies
4 guajillo chillies
6 cloves garlic, finely chopped
4 tsp ground cumin
2 Tbsp dried oregano
600ml (20½fl oz/2½ cups)
  beef stock
sea salt

8 warm tortillas, to serve
salsa of choice, to serve

fry

Preheat the oven to 150°C/300°F. Heat one tablespoon of the olive oil in a large frying pan and add half the diced beef. Brown for 4–5 minutes on each side on a medium to high heat, then remove and repeat with the remaining beef. Heat another tablespoon of the olive oil in a casserole dish (Dutch oven) and add the onions. Stir, then cover and leave to soften for 10 minutes, stirring occasionally. Toast the chillies in a separate, dry frying pan on a high heat for one minute on each side, then place in a bowl with just-boiled water and leave to soak, before chopping finely.

braise

Tip the soaking water into the frying pan used to brown the beef and allow to bubble for a few minutes, scraping the bottom of the pan to pick up all the flavours.

Add the chopped chillies, garlic, cumin and oregano to the softened onions and fry for a minute. Scrape into a blender, along with the beef stock, and blitz until smooth, then return to the casserole along with the browned beef and soaking water from the frying pan. Bring the mixture to the boil on a high heat, season with sea salt, then transfer immediately to the oven to braise for 3 hours.

shred

Shred the beef, and serve hot in warm tortillas with the salsa of your choice.

30 pork and purslane stew

serves ●●●●

prep ◔

cook x2 ◔

ingredients

600g (1lb 5oz) pork shoulder, cut into chunks
1 tsp black peppercorns
1 Tbsp olive oil
1 onion, roughly chopped
3 cloves garlic, finely chopped
1 jalapeño, roughly chopped
100g (3½oz) tomatillos (tinned is fine)
100g (3½oz) purslane, roughly chopped, few whole stems reserved to serve
sea salt

boil

Preheat your oven to 150°C/300°F. Place the pork shoulder in a large casserole dish (Dutch oven) with 1 litre (34fl oz/4 cups) water, three teaspoons of the sea salt and black peppercorns and bring to the boil. Transfer immediately to the oven and leave to cook for 2 hours.

fry

Heat the olive oil in a large frying pan, and fry the onion, garlic and jalapeño for 10 minutes, until softened. Add the chopped tomatillos and fry for a further 10 minutes.

blend

Once the pork has cooked, skim the scum from the broth and discard. Remove the pork, with a slotted spoon, and set aside. Strain 300ml (10fl oz/1¼ cups) of the hot broth through a sieve, then pour into a blender along with the onion and tomatillo mix and the purslane. Blitz until smooth, then return to a clean saucepan along with the pork.

simmer

Bring to the boil, then simmer on a low heat for 10 minutes. Season to taste with sea salt and serve hot with the reserved purslane.

chiles rellenos

(stuffed chillies)

serves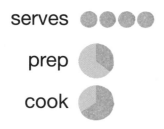

prep

cook

ingredients

4 poblano chillies

250g (9oz/1⅔ cups) oaxaca
   cheese or mozzarella, grated

1 litre (34fl oz/4 cups) vegetable
   oil, to fry

80g (2¾oz/⅔ cup) plain
   (all-purpose) flour

1 tsp sea salt

2 eggs, separated

pico de gallo (see page 51),
   to serve

roast

Arrange the poblano chillies in a roasting tin and
place under a medium-hot grill (broiler) for 10
minutes on each side until blackened.

steam

Transfer the chillies to a bowl and cover with
clingfilm (plastic wrap) for 5 minutes to allow
the skins to steam loose. Peel off the skins,
then carefully cut down one side without cutting
right through. Remove the seeds, then stuff with
the grated cheese.

heat

Heat the vegetable oil in a large frying pan until it
reaches 180°C/350°F, or until a cube of bread
dropped in turns golden within 30 seconds.

fry

Season the flour with salt. Dip each stuffed chilli
into the seasoned flour. Whisk the egg whites until
they form soft peaks, then gently fold in the yolks
and sea salt. Dip the floured chillies into the eggs,
then immediately drop into the hot oil. Fry for 2–3
minutes until golden-brown and crisp, and transfer
to a plate lined with kitchen paper.

serve

Serve immediately along with the pico de gallo.

32

cochinita pibil

(slow-cooked pork)

serves ●●●●

prep ◖

marinate **x3**

cook **x3**

ingredients

1 tsp cumin seeds
8 cloves
1 Tbsp dried oregano
250ml (8½fl oz/1 cup) orange
    juice (ideally freshly squeezed)
juice of 2 limes
6 cloves garlic, roughly chopped
1 onion, roughly chopped
50g (1¾oz) achiote paste
2 tsp sea salt
700g (1lb 9oz) pork shoulder,
    diced

8 tortillas or cooked rice, to serve
sour cream, to serve
escabeche de cebolla
    (see page 56), to serve

toast

Toast the cumin seeds, cloves and oregano in a
small frying pan on a low heat for 1–2 minutes, until
aromatic. Tip into a blender with the orange juice,
lime juice, garlic, onion, achiote paste and sea salt,
and blitz until smooth.

mix

Pour the mixture into a large bowl and combine
with the diced pork. Cover and refrigerate for at
least 3 hours, ideally overnight.

roast

Three hours before you are ready to eat, preheat
your oven to 150ºC/300ºF. Line the base of a large
casserole dish (Dutch oven) with a double layer of
foil. Tip in all the pork, along with the marinade, and
cover with another double layer of foil, clamping the
sides down well before covering and transferring to
the oven to roast for 3 hours.

serve

Remove the foil and shred the pork while hot.
Serve with tortillas or rice, sour cream and
escabeche de cebolla.

carnitas

(slow-cooked pork)

serves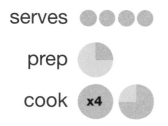

prep

cook x4

ingredients

1 onion, roughly sliced

6 cloves garlic, skin on, crushed

1 orange, roughly sliced

2 Tbsp oregano

2 bay leaves

1 cinnamon stick

1kg (2lb 3oz) boneless rolled
  pork shoulder

2 Tbsp sea salt

1 Tbsp ground cumin

1 Tbsp freshly ground black
  pepper

12 tortillas, to serve

salsa de piña picante (see page
  55), to serve

place

Preheat your oven to 150°C/300°F. Place half of
the sliced onion, garlic, orange slices, oregano, bay
leaves and cinnamon stick in the base of a small
lidded casserole dish (Dutch oven), small enough
to hold the pork shoulder snugly.

rub

Rub the pork with the sea salt, cumin and black
pepper and sit on top of the onion slices. Tuck
the remaining garlic, onion, orange, oregano and
bay leaves around the pork, place the lid on, and
transfer to the oven to cook for 4 hours.

shred

Once the pork is ready, remove it from the cooking
liquid and shred it with two forks and allow it to cool
down slightly. Pour the cooking liquid from the dish
into a jug and leave it to sit for 30 minutes to allow
the fat to rise to the surface.

fry

Pour a little of the fat over the shredded pork.
Heat a large frying pan and fry the pork in batches
on a medium heat for 10–15 minutes, stirring
occasionally. (The fat from the meat will help it to
crisp up.) Serve in tortillas alongside the salsa de
piña picante.

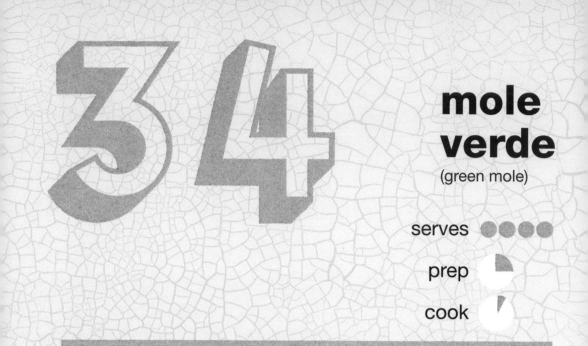

34

mole verde
(green mole)

serves ●●●●

prep ◔

cook ◐

ingredients
100g (3½oz/¾ cup) pumpkin
  seeds
200g tomatillos (tinned if
  not fresh)
½ small onion, roughly chopped
50g (1¾oz/1 cup) coriander
  (cilantro), roughly chopped
1 jalapeño, roughly chopped
2 cloves garlic, roughly chopped
2 Tbsp dried epazote
½ cos (romaine) lettuce, roughly
  chopped
150ml (5fl oz/⅔ cup) chicken
  stock, cooled
1–2 tsp sea salt

toast
Toast the pumpkin seeds in a dry pan for 4–5
minutes on a medium heat, until they begin to pop.

blend
Tip the seeds into a blender along with the
tomatillos, onion, coriander, jalapeño, garlic,
epazote, lettuce, cold chicken stock and sea
salt. Blitz until smooth.

serve
Taste and season with more sea salt as needed,
and serve with grilled chicken or pork.

35

huitla-coche
(corn smut)

serves ●●●●

prep

cook

ingredients
1 Tbsp olive oil
1 onion, finely sliced
2 cloves garlic, finely chopped
2 tsp dried epazote
200g (7oz) fresh or tinned
  huitlacoche (see page 8)
juice of ½ lime
sea salt

4 warm corn tortillas, to serve
100g (3½oz) queso fresco or
  feta, crumbled, to serve

heat
Heat the olive oil in a large frying pan and add the onions, garlic and epazote along with a pinch of sea salt. Lower the heat and soften for 10 minutes, stirring occasionally. Add the huitlacoche and stir-fry for 5–6 minutes, until cooked through.

serve
Season with the sea salt and lime juice to taste, then pile into the warm tortillas and top with the crumbled cheese.

36

chilli

serves ●●●●●●●

prep ◔

cook x3 ◑

ingredients

2 Tbsp olive oil
1 tsp cumin seeds
2 onions, roughly chopped
2 garlic cloves, finely chopped
800g (1lb 12oz) beef brisket, cut
   into 2.5-cm (1-in) chunks
350g (12½oz) pork shoulder, cut
   into 2.5-cm (1-in) chunks
1 ancho chilli
1 mulato chilli
2 guajillo chillies
2 tsp ground coriander
2 tsp ground cumin
2 tsp smoked paprika
1 x 400g (14oz) tin tomatoes
600ml (20fl oz/2½ cups) beef
   stock
large pinch sea salt
2 Tbsp chopped dark chocolate
   (70% cocoa solids minimum)

tortillas, to serve
sour cream, to serve

fry

Preheat your oven to 150°C/300°F. Heat one tablespoon of the olive oil in a large casserole dish (Dutch oven) and add the cumin seeds. Fry on a low heat for one minute until aromatic, then add the chopped onions and garlic. Soften for 10 minutes, stirring occasionally.

fry

Meanwhile, heat the other tablespoon of olive oil in a large frying pan and, working in small batches, brown the beef and pork in turn on a high heat for 2–3 minutes per side, until well browned. Add more oil if needed. Transfer the seared meat to a plate as you go.

soak

Toast the chillies in a dry frying pan for 2–3 minutes until aromatic. Place in a bowl and cover with just-boiled water. Leave to soak for 10 minutes, then drain. Remove the seeds and chop finely.

add

Once the onions in the casserole are softened, add the ground coriander, cumin, smoked paprika and finely chopped chillies. Stir-fry for 2–3 minutes until the spices are aromatic. Set aside.

➡ ➡ ➡

➡ ➡ ➡

Once the meat is all browned, add the tomatoes to the pan used to sear the meat, and cook on a high heat for 2–3 minutes, scraping up any sediment from the base of the pan with a wooden spoon.

mix

Tip the tomatoes and browned meat into the casserole dish with the onions and spices and pour in the beef stock. Add a large pinch of sea salt and stir well.

braise

Bring to the boil, cover, then transfer immediately to the oven to cook for 3 hours.

serve

Once cooked, shred the meat with two forks and stir the chocolate through the sauce. Season to taste with the sea salt. Serve with tortilla and sour cream.

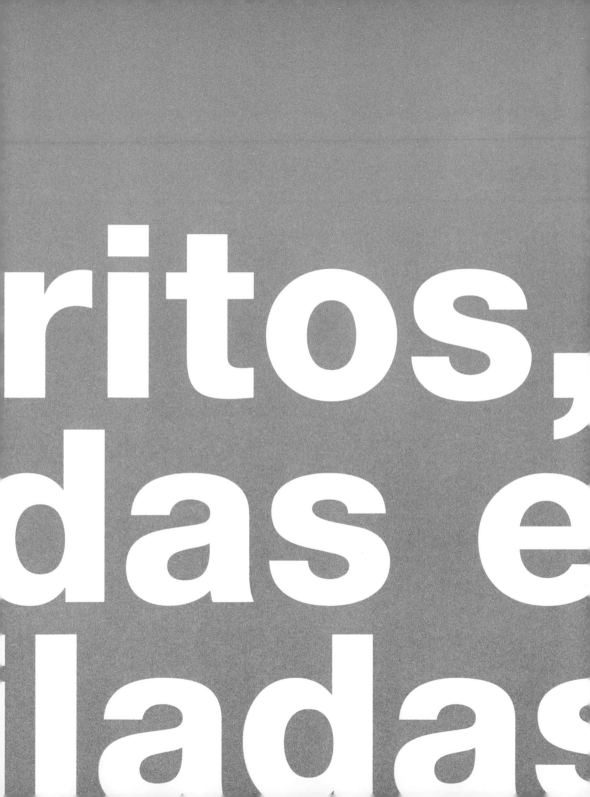

37

carne asada

(spiced steak)

serves

prep

marinate

cook

rest

ingredients

1 Tbsp coriander seeds
1 Tbsp cumin seeds
1 guajillo chilli
1 ancho chilli
1 pasilla chilli
zest and juice of 1 orange
zest and juice of 2 limes
2 Tbsp dark brown sugar
3 tsp sea salt
600g (1lb 5oz) flank or
    bavette steak

warm tortillas, to serve
coriander (cilantro), chopped,
    to serve

toast

Toast the seeds in a small, dry frying pan for 2–3 minutes, until aromatic. Allow to cool. Use a mortar and pestle (or coffee grinder) to grind the seeds to a fine powder.

blend

Toast the chillies in the same pan for 2–3 minutes on each side until aromatic. Deseed the chillies, then place the flesh in a blender or food processor, together with the ground cumin and coriander, the orange and lime zest and juice, the brown sugar and the sea salt. Blend until almost smooth, with a few pieces of chilli skin visible.

marinate

Reserve half of the mixture to use after the steaks have cooked. Pour the remaining marinade over the steak, cover and refrigerate for at least 1 hour.

grill

Take the steak out of the refrigerator 15 minutes before you intend to cook it. Heat a griddle pan until smoking hot, then grill (broil) the steaks for 3 minutes per side for medium rare, or 5–6 minutes per side for well done. When cooked to your liking, rest the steak on a plate, covered in foil, for 10 minutes.

serve

Serve the steak, sliced, in tortillas with the remaining marinade and the coriander.

38

tacos al pastor

serves ●●●●●

prep

marinate **1-3**

cook **x2**

ingredients

2 guajillo chillies
2 pasilla chillies
4 Tbsp white wine vinegar
120ml (4fl oz/½ cup) pineapple
   juice
4 cloves garlic
1 onion, roughly chopped
2 tsp ground cumin
25g (1oz) achiote paste
1kg (3lb 12oz) pork shoulder,
   cut into 1-cm (½-in) slices
2 tsp sea salt
2 Tbsp olive oil

tortillas, to serve
salsa de piña picante
   (see page 55), to serve

blend

Toast the chillies in a dry frying pan on a medium heat for 1–2 minutes on each side, until aromatic. Remove the stems and soak in just-boiled water for 15 minutes. Blitz the soaked chillies in a blender, along with the vinegar, pineapple juice, garlic, onion, cumin and achiote paste, until smooth. Mix the pork slices well with the marinade in a shallow dish, and leave to marinate for 1–3 hours.

roast

Preheat your oven to 150°C/300°F. Line a roasting tin with foil, spread the pork slices in an even layer over the base. Top with another layer of foil, and scrunch down tightly. Roast in the oven for 1 hour and 30 minutes. Turn the heat up to 200°C /400°F, remove the foil and roast for 30 minutes.

serve

Serve the pork hot in warm tortillas along with the salsa de piña picante.

39

chicken tinga

serves

prep

cook

ingredients

1 guajillo chilli
1 Tbsp olive oil
300g (10½oz) skinless, boneless
    chicken thighs
1 onion, finely sliced
2 cloves garlic
1 Tbsp oregano
2 heaped tsp flaked chipotle
200g (7oz) chopped fresh or
    tinned tomatoes
3–4 tomatillos (approx. 60g)
sea salt

4–6 tortillas, to serve
1 little gem lettuce (per person),
    shredded, to serve
100g (3½oz/⅓ cup) sour cream,
    to serve
salsa of choice, to serve

heat

Halve the chilli and toast in a dry frying-pan over
a medium-heat for 1–2 minutes until aromatic,
then place in a bowl and cover with the just-boiled
water. Heat the olive oil in the same frying pan and
brown the chicken for 5 minutes on each side,
then remove with a slotted spoon to a plate.

simmer

In the same pan, fry the onion, garlic, oregano,
chipotle and a pinch of sea salt for 10 minutes,
until softened. Place in a blender along with the
tomatoes, tomatillos, soaked chilli and soaking
water. Blitz until smooth. Return to the pan along
with the chicken. Simmer on a very low heat,
partially covered, for 30 minutes.

serve

Shred the chicken, and serve hot in tortillas
with sliced lettuce, sour cream and salsa
of choice.

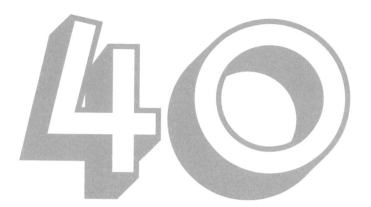

40 fish tacos

serves

prep

cook

ingredients

150g (5½oz/scant 1¼ cups)
    plain (all-purpose) flour
1½ tsp baking powder
1 tsp sea salt
200ml (7fl oz/scant 1 cup) cold,
    dark Mexican beer
500g (1lb 2oz) cod or other firm
    white fish, cut into 2.5 x 5-cm
    (1 x 2-in) chunks

1 litre (34fl oz/4 cups)
    vegetable oil, to fry

taco shells, to serve
2 cos (romaine) lettuces, sliced,
    to serve
1 red onion, thinly sliced,
    to serve
salsa of choice, to serve

prep

Prepare the lettuce and onion first, and any
accompanying salsas, as the fish must be eaten
as soon as it is cooked.

mix

Mix together the flour, baking powder and
sea salt in a mixing bowl.

heat

Pour the oil into a large frying pan, no more than
half full, and heat to 180ºC/350ºF, or until a cube
of bread turns golden within 30 seconds.

dip

Just before you are ready begin frying, whisk the
beer through the flour mixture and dip the fish into
the batter. Stir briefly to coat, then drain each piece
against the side of the bowl before carefully sliding
it into the hot oil. You should be able to fry about
four pieces of fish at a time. Deep-fry the fish for
2–3 minutes until golden-brown and crisp, then
transfer to a plate lined with kitchen paper while
you continue with the rest.

serve

Serve the fish immediately with the tacos, lettuce
and onion. You can also serve it with the pico de
gallo (see page 51).

41 campechano

(steak taco)

serves ●●●●●

prep ▶

marinate ●

cook ▶

ingredients

400g (14oz) sirloin steak, cut into
1-cm (½-in) slices
2 Tbsp olive oil
1 Tbsp oregano (preferably
Mexican)
½ onion, finely sliced
1 clove garlic, minced
½ tsp sea salt
125g (4½oz) chorizo, diced

warm tortillas, to serve
salsa molcateje (see page
64), to serve

mix

Place the steak in a bowl and mix with one
tablespoon of the olive oil, the oregano, onion,
garlic and sea salt. Cover and refrigerate for at
least 1 hour.

fry

When you are ready to eat heat the remaining olive
oil in a frying pan and fry the chorizo on a medium
heat for 3–4 minutes, until cooked through.

fry

Turn the heat up to very high and then add the
marinated steak and onions. Stir-fry very quickly
for 45 seconds for rare, 1 minute 30 seconds for
medium, or 2–3 minutes for well done.

serve

Pile into tortillas with salsa and serve hot.

42

tacos de papa

(fried potato tacos)

serves ●●●●

prep ◕

cook ◔

ingredients

400g (14oz) medium potatoes,
  peeled, halved and cooked
1 tsp ground cumin
¼ onion, finely chopped
1 jalapeño, finely chopped
4 tortillas
2 tablespoons vegetable oil
sea salt

½ red onion, finely chopped
1 avocado, cut into 1-cm
  (½-in) cubes
65g (2¼oz) cherry tomatoes,
  quartered then halved
juice of ½ lime
10g (¼oz/scant ¼ cup)
  coriander (cilantro), roughly
  chopped

boil

Place the potatoes in a saucepan and cover with cold water. Bring to the boil, then simmer for 25–30 minutes until cooked through. Drain and allow to cool.

mix

Meanwhile, make the guacamole by combining the red onion, avocado, tomatoes, lime juice, coriander and one teaspoon of sea salt in a bowl.

fold

Mash the potatoes with the cumin, onion, 2 teaspoons of sea salt and the jalapeño. Take a quarter of the mixture and spread it over one half of a tortilla, before folding the tortilla in half over the potato filling. Repeat with the remaining tortillas.

fry

Heat a little of the vegetable oil in a large frying pan and, working with two at a time, fry the tortillas for 3 minutes per side on a medium-heat, until crisp and golden-brown. Transfer to a plate lined with kitchen paper, add a little more oil to the pan and repeat with the remaining tortillas.

serve

Serve hot with the guacamole alongside.

enchiladas

ingredients

2 ancho chillies
3 guajillo chillies
2 cloves garlic
1 tsp oregano
5 Tbsp olive oil
1 Tbsp plain (all-purpose) flour
250ml (8½fl oz/1 cup) hot
  chicken stock
8 tortillas
1 red onion, finely chopped
300g (10½oz/2 cups) feta,
  crumbled, plus extra to serve
200g (7oz/scant 1 cup) ricotta
90g (3oz/⅓ cup) sour cream,
  to serve
sea salt

2 spring onions (scallions),
  finely chopped, to serve

toast

Preheat the oven to 200°C/400°F. Place the chillies in a dry saucepan and toast over a medium heat for 2–3 minutes, until aromatic. Deseed the chillies, transfer to a bowl, cover with just-boiled water and leave to soak for 20 minutes.

blend

Pour the soaked chillies and the soaking water into a blender with the garlic and oregano. Blitz until you have a smooth purée.

heat

Heat 1 tablespoon of the olive oil in a small saucepan and add the flour. Stir for a minute on a low heat, then add the chilli purée. Stir to combine, then add the chicken stock and whisk until smooth. Bring to the boil and simmer for 5 minutes. Taste and season with sea salt.

serves ●●●●

prep

cook

fry
Meanwhile, heat 1 tablespoon of the olive oil in a large frying pan and fry the tortillas on a low heat for a minute on each side, until golden-brown, but still soft, adding more oil as needed in between tortillas. Set aside.

mix
Mix together the red onion, feta and ricotta in a bowl. To assemble the enchiladas, spread 2 tablespoons of the chilli sauce over each tortilla, top with 2 heaped tablespoons of the cheese and onion mixture, then roll up and place in a baking dish, seam side down. Repeat with the remaining tortillas. Spread the remaining sauce over the top of the tortillas, and bake in the preheated oven for 20 minutes.

serve
Top with the sour cream, extra feta and spring onions and serve hot.

44

tortillas

makes

prep

cook

ingredients

200g (7oz/1⅔ cups) plain (all-purpose) flour, plus extra to dust
½ tsp sea salt
½ tsp baking powder
2 Tbsp olive oil

mix

Mix the flour, sea salt and baking powder together in a large bowl, before adding the olive oil and 100ml (3½fl oz/scant 1 cup) water. Work together to form a smooth dough and knead briefly for 3–4 minutes. Place the dough back in the bowl, cover and rest for 10 minutes.

divide

Divide the dough into 8 pieces, and cover. On a floured work surface, roll out each ball into a round. In order to keep them soft don't roll them too thinly, no larger than 15–17cm (6–6¾in).

heat

Heat a large frying pan on a medium heat, and cook each tortilla for 1 minute per side until dark spots appear. Continue until all the tortillas are cooked. If not using immediately, wrap them in foil and warm through in a hot oven for 10 minutes before eating.

(desserts)

churros

(fried choux pastry with
chocolate sauce)

serves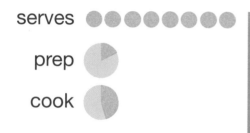

prep

cook

ingredients

160g (5½oz/1⅔ cups) plain
   (all-purpose) flour
½ tsp baking powder
pinch sea salt
80g (2¾oz/⅓ cup) butter
3 eggs

100g (3½oz/scant ½ cup) caster
   (superfine) sugar
1 heaped tsp cinnamon powder

1 litre (34fl oz/4 cups)
   vegetable oil, to fry

500ml (17fl oz/2 cups) double
   (heavy) cream
pinch chilli powder
200g (7oz/1⅓ cups) dark
   chocolate (70% cocoa solids
   minimum), chopped

equipment

1 x large snowflake/star-shaped
   nozzle
1 x piping bag

mix

Sift the flour, baking powder and sea salt together in a large bowl and mix well. In a large saucepan, heat 250ml (8½fl oz/1 cup) water and butter until just boiling. Lower the heat, tip in the flour mixture and beat together quickly until you have a stiff dough that comes away cleanly from the sides of the pan. Tip the dough back into the bowl, spread it thinly around the sides and leave it to cool for 5 minutes.

mix

Meanwhile, in a separate bowl, mix together the sugar and cinnamon. Set aside.

beat

One at a time, beat the eggs into the cooled dough, mixing until fully incorporated before beating in the next. You may need to use a whisk in conjunction with a wooden spoon – the mixture will come together eventually.

rest

Cut the tip from a piping bag and fit the star shaped nozzle. Spoon in half of the prepared dough and set aside to rest for at least 10 minutes.

heat

Heat the oil in a large saucepan, making sure to fill it no more than two-thirds full, and bring the temperature up to 180°C/350°F. While the oil is

➡➡➡

➡➡➡
heating up, in a separate, small saucepan heat the cream with the chilli powder. Just as it begins to boil, lower the heat and add the chopped chocolate. Stir continuously until the chocolate has melted. Turn off the heat, cover and keep the sauce in a warm place.

fry

Preheat your oven to 50°C/120°F. Once the oil has reached the correct temperature, carefully pipe hoops of dough straight into the hot oil, using the side of the pan to 'cut' the end of each hoop. It's best to cook just three to four churros at a time as they'll cook more evenly. Fry the churros for 1½–2 minutes on each side, until golden-brown and evenly crisp all over. Use a slotted spoon to transfer the churros one by one to a plate lined with kitchen paper, carefully draining the excess oil into the pan beforehand.

toss

Toss the churros in the bowl with the cinnamon sugar within a minute of removing them from the pan, and keep the sugared churros in the oven to keep warm.

serve

Repeat, until you have used up all the dough, and serve the churros hot with the chocolate sauce to dip.

flan de casero

(creme caramel)

ingredients

100g (3½oz/scant ½ cup) caster (superfine) sugar
400ml (13½fl oz/1⅔ cups) full-fat (whole) milk
1 x 400g tin (14oz/1¼ cups) condensed milk
4 eggs, plus 2 egg yolks
1 tsp vanilla extract

equipment

1 x 20-cm (8-in) tart tin

heat

Preheat the oven to 180°C/350°F. Tip the sugar into a heavy-based frying pan, and heat gently without stirring, until the sugar melts and turns dark amber in colour. Tilt the pan to help the sugar to melt evenly. Check that the syrup is the right temperature by dropping a teaspoon of hot water in – it will immediately form a brittle amber thread. Pour the caramel into the base of the tart tin.

whisk

Meanwhile, heat the milk and condensed milk together in a saucepan on a low heat until it just comes to the boil. Remove from the heat. In a bowl, whisk together the eggs, egg yolks and vanilla extract, then, whisking continuously, pour in the hot milk. Allow the custard to cool for 5 minutes, then gently pour it over the caramel in the tart tin. For a super smooth set, sieve the warm custard before pouring it into the tart tin.

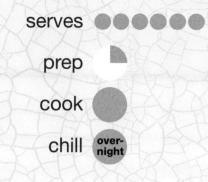

serves ●●●●●●

prep

cook

chill over-night

bake

Place the tart into a large roasting tin and fill three-quarters of the way up the sides of the tart tin with just-boiled water. Carefully transfer to the oven and bake for 50 minutes to 1 hour, until lightly browned and set. It will be firm to the touch but still have a slight wobble in the middle.

chill

Remove from the oven, leave to cool down completely, then transfer to the refrigerator to chill overnight.

serve

Just before you are ready to serve, place your serving plate over the flan tin, then quickly and carefully flip it upside down. Remove the tin, and serve with fresh fruit.

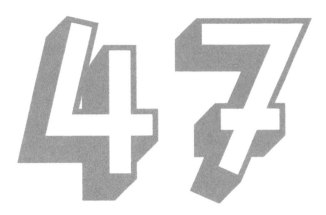

pastel de tres leches

(three milk cake)

ingredients

225g (8oz/1¾ cups) plain
   (all-purpose) flour
1 tsp baking powder
125g (4½oz/scant ⅔ cups)
   caster (superfine) sugar
75g (2¾oz/generous ¼ cup)
   butter, softened
1 tsp vanilla extract
4 eggs, separated
100ml (3½fl oz/scant ½ cup)
   full-fat (whole) milk

200ml (210g/7½oz⅔ cup)
   condensed milk
170ml (5½fl oz/⅔ cup)
   evaporated milk
50ml (1¾fl oz/¼ cup) double
   (heavy) cream

➡ ➡ ➡

heat

Preheat the oven to 180°C/350°F. Grease a 20cm (8in) square or round cake tin and line with baking (parchment) paper.

mix

Sift the flour and baking powder together in a bowl, and set aside. Beat together the sugar and butter until light and fluffy. Add the vanilla extract and then, one by one, mix in the egg yolks. Add the milk and fold through the flour and baking powder.

beat

In a separate bowl, with a very clean electric whisk, beat the egg whites together until they form soft peaks. Beat 2 tablespoons of the whisked egg whites through the cake batter to lighten it. Then gently fold in the remaining egg whites, taking care not to knock all the air from the mixture.

bake

Scrape into the prepared cake tin, and bake in the centre of the oven for 35–40 minutes, until

➡ ➡ ➡
200ml (7fl oz/scant 1 cup)
  double (heavy) cream, to
  serve
strawberries, kiwis or other fruit,
  to serve

the cake is golden-brown, and firm to the touch.
Remove and turn out onto a wire rack to cool.

simmer

Meanwhile, pour the condensed milk, evaporated
milk and cream into a large saucepan and bring to
the boil, stirring constantly. Keep a close eye on it
as it will want to bubble over. Lower the heat and
simmer for 10 minutes, then remove from the heat
and leave to cool.

pour

Gently return the cake back to its lined tin, and
puncture all over with a fork. Pour the cooled milk
mixture all over the cake until it is saturated and
leave for at least 30 minutes to soak.

serve

For the topping, whip the double cream until it
forms very soft peaks. Spread over the cake, and
top with fruit of your choice before serving.

paletas

(ice pops)

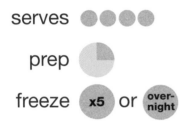

serves ●●●●

prep

freeze  x5 or over-night

ingredients

150g (5½oz/⅔ cup) caster
  (superfine) sugar
150g (5½oz/generous 1 cup)
  blackberries
110ml (4fl oz/scant ½ cup) lime
  juice, approx. 4 limes

equipment

4 x 100ml (3½fl oz) ice pop
  moulds

heat

Place the sugar, half of the blackberries and 50ml
(1¾fl oz/scant ¼ cup) water in a saucepan on a
low heat, and stir for 3–4 minutes until the sugar
has dissolved. Squash a couple of the blackberries
to get a nice colour through the syrup.

mix

Take the syrup off the heat and pour into a
measuring jug with the lime juice: you should
have 300ml (10 fl oz/1¼ cups) of liquid. Add
the remaining blackberries, and enough water
to bring the total amount of liquid to 400ml
(14fl oz/1⅔ cups). Stir well, then leave to cool
to room temperature.

freeze

Pour the juice into the ice pop moulds, making
sure to leave a little space at the top for the ice to
expand, and freeze for 5 hours, or ideally overnight.

serve

When ready to eat, depending on your moulds,
either hold the ice pop moulds under hot running
water for 30 seconds, or dip the tray into a bowl
of hot water for a few seconds, before pulling the
paletas out. Serve immediately.

arroz
con leche
(rice pudding)

serves ●●●●●

prep

cook

ingredients
200g (7oz/1 cup) medium or
   short-grain rice
1.2 litres (41fl oz/scant 5 cups)
   full-fat (whole) milk
1 cinnamon stick
2 strips lemon peel
1 x 400g (14oz/1¼ cups) tin
   condensed milk

pinch cinnamon powder, to
   serve

simmer
Rinse the rice under cold running water, pour the
milk into a saucepan, add the cinnamon stick and
lemon peel and bring to the boil. Add the rice,
reduce the heat and simmer for 20 minutes. Stir
occasionally to prevent the rice from sticking.

mix
Strain the rice through a sieve, reserving the milk,
and then return the rice to the pan. Stir in the
condensed milk and 200ml (7fl oz/scant 1 cup) of
the reserved milk and continue to simmer, partially
covered, for 20 minutes. Stir every 5 minutes or so.

serve
Serve the rice pudding hot, sprinkled with
cinnamon. If not serving immediately, the
pudding will thicken as it sits, so stir through
the reserved milk a little at a time to adjust the
texture to your taste.

sopa-
pillas

(fried pastry)

ingredients

225g (8oz/1¾ cups) plain
   (all-purpose) flour
1 tsp baking powder
1 tsp sea salt
2 tsp caster (superfine) sugar
150ml (5fl oz/⅔ cup) full-fat
   (whole) milk

75g (2¾oz/⅓ cup) caster
   (superfine) sugar, plus
   1½ tsp cinnamon powder
   or honey

1 litre (34fl oz/4 cups) vegetable
   oil, to fry

mix

Sift the flour and baking powder into a large bowl.
Stir through the sea salt and the 2 teaspoons
of sugar. Add the milk and bring the ingredients
together with a fork, then use your hands to form a
sticky dough. Knead together briefly for 2 minutes,
until smooth, then return to the bowl. Cover and
leave to rest for 15 minutes.

mix

Mix together the 75g of sugar and the cinnamon
(or honey) in a wide bowl and set aside.

heat

Heat the vegetable oil in a large saucepan to
180°C/350°F, or until a cube of bread dropped in
fizzes and turns brown within 30 seconds.

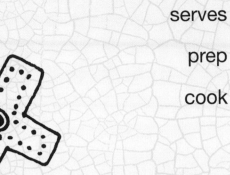

serves ●●●●●

prep ◖

cook ◗

fry

On a lightly floured surface, roll out the dough into a large rectangle, 2mm (1/15in) thick. Cut the dough into 6 x 4cm (2½ x 1½in) rectangles. Carefully drop four or five of the pastry pieces into the hot oil; they will sink to the base of the pan before rising to the surface. To help them to form their characteristic pillow shape, flip each one gently with a slotted spoon until it puffs up, then fry for 20–30 seconds per side until golden-brown.

coat

Drain each sopapilla well with the slotted spoon against the side of the pan, then drop immediately into the bowl of cinnamon sugar. Spoon plenty of sugar over each to coat, then transfer to a plate lined with kitchen paper as you continue frying the rest of the sopapillas.

serve

These are best eaten within seconds of being fried, so make sure that anyone who wants to eat them is nearby.

index

publishing director: Sarah Lavelle
creative director: Helen Lewis
junior commissioning editor: Romilly Morgan
design and art direction: Claire Rochford
recipe developer and food stylist: Rukmini Iyer
photographer: Kim Lightbody
illustrator: Juriko Kosaka
prop stylist: Alexander Breeze
production: Tom Moore, Vincent Smith

First published in 2016 by
Quadrille Publishing
Pentagon House
52–54 Southwark Street
London SE1 1UN
www.quadrille.co.uk
www.quadrille.com

Quadrille is an imprint of Hardie Grant
www.hardiegrant.com.au

Text © 2016 Quadrille Publishing
Photography © 2016 Kim Lightbody
Illustration © 2016 Juriko Kosaka
Design and layout © 2016 Quadrille Publishing

The rights of the author have been asserted. All rights reserved. No part of this book shall be reproduced, stored in a retrieval system, or transmitted by any means – electronic, mechanical, photocopying, recording, or otherwise – without written permission from the publisher.

Cataloguing in Publication Data: a catalogue record for this book is available from the British Library.

ISBN: 978 184949 880 7

Printed in China

Thank you to all the owners and staff who allowed us to shoot photographs in the following locations: Barrio Central in Poland Street W1F, El Camion in Brewer Street W1F, Seven Sisters Market N15 and Tamali – Mexican Eating at Maltby Street Market SE1.

Note: follow the standard safety tips for deep frying – fill the pan no more than half full with oil, keep it towards the back of the stove, do not leave it unattended, and do not overcrowd the pan, or it will bubble over. Once you have finished frying, turn off the heat and do not attempt to move the pan of oil until it has completely cooled down.